Dream NOTES

A special space dedicated for journaling dreams before turning them into goals. Use this Daily *Dream* Journal to jot down dream notes, capture thoughts, daily reflections, daily goals and daily to do's.

Printed in the USA by A2Z Books, LLC. Copyright by Lisa WalkerHolloway of JMC Career Solutions & Consulting LLC. All rights reserved. This Journal or any portion thereof may not be reproduced or used in any manner whatsoever without the express written permission of the publisher except for the use of brief quotations in book review Printed in the United States. First Printing ISBN 978-1-943284-64-1
www.A2ZBookspublishing.net

MY DAILY *Dream* JOURNAL

_____

_____

_____

TODAY: _____

NOTES:

What did you dream about last night?

Today's " Get It Done" List

Top 3 Goals for the Day

End of the Day Reflections

TODAY: _____

NOTES:

What did you dream about last night?

Today's " Get It Done" List

Top 3 Goals for the Day

End of the Day Reflections

TODAY: _____	NOTES:

What did you dream about last night?

Today's " Get It Done" List

End of the Day Reflections

Top 3 Goals for the Day

TODAY: _____

What did you dream about last night?
_____
_____
_____
_____
_____
_____
_____

Today's " Get It Done" List
_____
_____
_____
_____
_____
_____
_____

Top 3 Goals for the Day
_____
_____
_____
_____
_____
_____
_____

NOTES:
_____
_____
_____
_____
_____
_____
_____
_____
_____
_____
_____

End of the Day Reflections
_____
_____
_____
_____
_____
_____
_____
_____
_____
_____
_____

TODAY: _____   NOTES:

What did you dream about last night?
_____
_____
_____
_____
_____
_____
_____

Today's " Get It Done" List
_____
_____
_____
_____
_____
_____
_____

End of the Day Reflections

Top 3 Goals for the Day
_____
_____
_____
_____
_____
_____
_____
_____

TODAY: _____

NOTES:

What did you dream about last night?
_____
_____
_____
_____
_____
_____
_____

Today's " Get It Done" List
_____
_____
_____
_____
_____
_____
_____

End of the Day Reflections

Top 3 Goals for the Day
_____
_____
_____
_____
_____
_____
_____

TODAY: _____

NOTES:

What did you dream about last night?

Today's " Get It Done" List

Top 3 Goals for the Day

End of the Day Reflections

TODAY: _____   NOTES:

What did you dream about last night?
_____
_____
_____
_____
_____
_____
_____

Today's " Get It Done" List
_____
_____
_____
_____
_____
_____
_____

Top 3 Goals for the Day
_____
_____
_____
_____
_____
_____
_____

End of the Day Reflections

TODAY: _____   NOTES:

What did you dream about last night?
_____
_____
_____
_____
_____
_____
_____

Today's " Get It Done" List
_____
_____
_____
_____
_____
_____
_____

End of the Day Reflections

Top 3 Goals for the Day
_____
_____
_____
_____
_____
_____
_____

TODAY: _____

NOTES:

What did you dream about last night?

Today's " Get It Done" List

Top 3 Goals for the Day

End of the Day Reflections

TODAY: _____

NOTES:

What did you dream about last night?

Today's " Get It Done" List

Top 3 Goals for the Day

End of the Day Reflections

TODAY: _____

NOTES:

What did you dream about last night?
_____
_____
_____
_____
_____
_____
_____

Today's " Get It Done" List
_____
_____
_____
_____
_____
_____
_____

Top 3 Goals for the Day
_____
_____
_____
_____
_____
_____

End of the Day Reflections

TODAY: _____ NOTES:

What did you dream about last night?
_____
_____
_____
_____
_____
_____
_____
_____

Today's " Get It Done" List
_____
_____
_____
_____
_____
_____
_____

End of the Day Reflections

Top 3 Goals for the Day
_____
_____
_____
_____
_____

TODAY: _____   NOTES:

What did you dream about last night?
_____
_____
_____
_____
_____
_____
_____

Today's " Get It Done" List
_____
_____
_____
_____
_____
_____
_____

End of the Day Reflections

Top 3 Goals for the Day
_____
_____
_____
_____
_____
_____
_____

TODAY: _____

NOTES:

What did you dream about last night?

Today's " Get It Done" List

Top 3 Goals for the Day

End of the Day Reflections

TODAY: _____

NOTES:
_____
_____
_____
_____
_____
_____
_____
_____
_____
_____
_____
_____
_____

What did you dream about last night?
_____
_____
_____
_____
_____
_____
_____

Today's " Get It Done" List
_____
_____
_____
_____
_____
_____
_____

End of the Day Reflections
_____
_____
_____
_____
_____
_____
_____
_____
_____

Top 3 Goals for the Day
_____
_____
_____
_____
_____
_____

TODAY: _____   NOTES:

What did you dream about last night?
_____
_____
_____
_____
_____
_____
_____

Today's " Get It Done" List
_____
_____
_____
_____
_____
_____
_____

End of the Day Reflections

Top 3 Goals for the Day
_____
_____
_____
_____
_____
_____

TODAY: _____   NOTES:

What did you dream about last night?
_____
_____
_____
_____
_____
_____
_____
_____

Today's " Get It Done" List
_____
_____
_____
_____
_____
_____
_____

End of the Day Reflections

Top 3 Goals for the Day
_____
_____
_____
_____
_____
_____
_____

TODAY: _____   NOTES:

What did you dream about last night?
_____
_____
_____
_____
_____
_____
_____

Today's " Get It Done" List
_____
_____
_____
_____
_____
_____
_____
_____

Top 3 Goals for the Day
_____
_____
_____
_____
_____
_____
_____

(Notes lines on right side)

End of the Day Reflections

TODAY: _____

What did you dream about last night?
_____
_____
_____
_____
_____
_____
_____

Today's " Get It Done" List
_____
_____
_____
_____
_____
_____
_____

Top 3 Goals for the Day
_____
_____
_____
_____
_____
_____
_____

NOTES:
_____
_____
_____
_____
_____
_____
_____
_____
_____
_____

End of the Day Reflections
_____
_____
_____
_____
_____
_____
_____
_____
_____

TODAY: _____   NOTES:

What did you dream about last night?
_____
_____
_____
_____
_____
_____
_____

Today's " Get It Done" List
_____
_____
_____
_____
_____
_____
_____

Top 3 Goals for the Day
_____
_____
_____
_____
_____
_____
_____
_____

End of the Day Reflections

TODAY: _____

NOTES:

What did you dream about last night?
_____
_____
_____
_____
_____
_____
_____

Today's " Get It Done" List
_____
_____
_____
_____
_____
_____
_____

End of the Day Reflections

Top 3 Goals for the Day

TODAY: _____   NOTES:

What did you dream about last night?

Today's " Get It Done" List

End of the Day Reflections

Top 3 Goals for the Day

TODAY: _____

NOTES:

What did you dream about last night?

Today's " Get It Done" List

Top 3 Goals for the Day

End of the Day Reflections

TODAY: _____   NOTES:

What did you dream about last night?
_____
_____
_____
_____
_____
_____
_____

Today's " Get It Done" List
_____
_____
_____
_____
_____
_____
_____

End of the Day Reflections

Top 3 Goals for the Day
_____
_____
_____
_____
_____
_____
_____

TODAY: _____

NOTES:

What did you dream about last night?
_____
_____
_____
_____
_____
_____
_____

Today's " Get It Done" List
_____
_____
_____
_____
_____
_____

End of the Day Reflections

Top 3 Goals for the Day
_____
_____
_____
_____
_____
_____

TODAY: _____

NOTES:

What did you dream about last night?
_____
_____
_____
_____
_____
_____
_____

Today's " Get It Done" List
_____
_____
_____
_____
_____
_____
_____

Top 3 Goals for the Day
_____
_____
_____
_____
_____
_____
_____
_____

_____
_____
_____
_____
_____
_____
_____
_____
_____
_____
_____
_____
_____

End of the Day Reflections
_____
_____
_____
_____
_____
_____
_____
_____
_____
_____
_____

TODAY: _____   NOTES:

What did you dream about last night?
_____
_____
_____
_____
_____
_____
_____

Today's " Get It Done" List
_____
_____
_____
_____
_____
_____
_____

Top 3 Goals for the Day
_____
_____
_____
_____
_____
_____
_____

End of the Day Reflections

TODAY: _____   NOTES:

What did you dream about last night?

Today's " Get It Done" List

End of the Day Reflections

Top 3 Goals for the Day

TODAY: _____   NOTES:

What did you dream about last night?
_____
_____
_____
_____
_____
_____
_____

Today's " Get It Done" List
_____
_____
_____
_____
_____
_____
_____

End of the Day Reflections

Top 3 Goals for the Day
_____
_____
_____
_____
_____

TODAY: _____   NOTES:

What did you dream about last night?
_____
_____
_____
_____
_____
_____
_____

Today's " Get It Done" List
_____
_____
_____
_____
_____
_____
_____

End of the Day Reflections

Top 3 Goals for the Day
_____
_____
_____
_____
_____
_____

TODAY: _____   NOTES:

What did you dream about last night?
_____
_____
_____
_____
_____
_____
_____

Today's " Get It Done" List
_____
_____
_____
_____
_____
_____
_____

Top 3 Goals for the Day
_____
_____
_____
_____
_____
_____
_____

End of the Day Reflections

TODAY: _____   NOTES:

What did you dream about last night?

Today's " Get It Done" List

Top 3 Goals for the Day

End of the Day Reflections

TODAY: _____   NOTES:

What did you dream about last night?
_____
_____
_____
_____
_____
_____
_____

Today's " Get It Done" List
_____
_____
_____
_____
_____
_____

End of the Day Reflections

Top 3 Goals for the Day
_____
_____
_____
_____
_____
_____
_____

TODAY: _____   NOTES:

What did you dream about last night?
_____
_____
_____
_____
_____
_____
_____

Today's " Get It Done" List
_____
_____
_____
_____
_____
_____
_____

Top 3 Goals for the Day
_____
_____
_____
_____
_____
_____
_____

End of the Day Reflections

TODAY: _____

NOTES:

What did you dream about last night?

Today's " Get It Done" List

Top 3 Goals for the Day

End of the Day Reflections

TODAY: _____   NOTES:

What did you dream about last night?

Today's " Get It Done" List

Top 3 Goals for the Day

End of the Day Reflections

TODAY: _____

NOTES:

What did you dream about last night?

Today's " Get It Done" List

Top 3 Goals for the Day

End of the Day Reflections

TODAY: _____   NOTES:

What did you dream about last night?
_____
_____
_____
_____
_____
_____
_____

Today's " Get It Done" List
_____
_____
_____
_____
_____
_____
_____

Top 3 Goals for the Day
_____
_____
_____
_____
_____
_____
_____

End of the Day Reflections

TODAY: _____   NOTES:

What did you dream about last night?
_____
_____
_____
_____
_____
_____
_____

Today's " Get It Done" List
_____
_____
_____
_____
_____
_____

End of the Day Reflections

Top 3 Goals for the Day
_____
_____
_____
_____
_____
_____
_____

TODAY: _____   NOTES:

What did you dream about last night?
_____
_____
_____
_____
_____
_____
_____

Today's " Get It Done" List
_____
_____
_____
_____
_____
_____
_____

End of the Day Reflections

Top 3 Goals for the Day
_____
_____
_____
_____
_____
_____
_____

TODAY: _____   NOTES:

What did you dream about last night?
_____
_____
_____
_____
_____
_____
_____
_____

Today's " Get It Done" List
_____
_____
_____
_____
_____
_____
_____

End of the Day Reflections

Top 3 Goals for the Day
_____
_____
_____
_____
_____
_____
_____

TODAY: _____   NOTES:

What did you dream about last night?
_____
_____
_____
_____
_____
_____
_____

Today's " Get It Done" List
_____
_____
_____
_____
_____
_____
_____

End of the Day Reflections

Top 3 Goals for the Day
_____
_____
_____
_____
_____
_____
_____

TODAY: _____ NOTES:

What did you dream about last night?

Today's " Get It Done" List

End of the Day Reflections

Top 3 Goals for the Day

TODAY: _____   NOTES:

What did you dream about last night?
_____
_____
_____
_____
_____
_____
_____

Today's " Get It Done" List
_____
_____
_____
_____
_____
_____
_____

Top 3 Goals for the Day
_____
_____
_____
_____
_____
_____
_____
_____

End of the Day Reflections
_____
_____
_____
_____
_____
_____
_____

TODAY: _____

NOTES:

What did you dream about last night?

Today's " Get It Done" List

End of the Day Reflections

Top 3 Goals for the Day

TODAY: _____   NOTES:

What did you dream about last night?
_____
_____
_____
_____
_____
_____
_____

Today's " Get It Done" List
_____
_____
_____
_____
_____
_____
_____

End of the Day Reflections

Top 3 Goals for the Day
_____
_____
_____
_____
_____
_____
_____

TODAY: _____

NOTES:

What did you dream about last night?
_____
_____
_____
_____
_____
_____
_____
_____

Today's " Get It Done" List
_____
_____
_____
_____
_____
_____
_____

Top 3 Goals for the Day
_____
_____
_____
_____
_____
_____
_____

End of the Day Reflections

TODAY: _____   NOTES:

What did you dream about last night?
_____
_____
_____
_____
_____
_____
_____

Today's " Get It Done" List
_____
_____
_____
_____
_____
_____
_____

End of the Day Reflections

Top 3 Goals for the Day
_____
_____
_____
_____
_____
_____

TODAY: _____   NOTES:

What did you dream about last night?
_____
_____
_____
_____
_____
_____
_____

Today's " Get It Done" List
_____
_____
_____
_____
_____
_____
_____

End of the Day Reflections

Top 3 Goals for the Day
_____
_____
_____
_____
_____
_____
_____

TODAY: _____   NOTES:

What did you dream about last night?
_____
_____
_____
_____
_____
_____

Today's " Get It Done" List
_____
_____
_____
_____
_____

End of the Day Reflections

Top 3 Goals for the Day
_____
_____
_____
_____
_____
_____

TODAY: _____   NOTES:

What did you dream about last night?
_____
_____
_____
_____
_____
_____
_____

Today's " Get It Done" List
_____
_____
_____
_____
_____
_____

End of the Day Reflections

Top 3 Goals for the Day
_____
_____
_____
_____
_____
_____

TODAY: _____ NOTES:

What did you dream about last night?
_____
_____
_____
_____
_____
_____
_____

Today's " Get It Done" List
_____
_____
_____
_____
_____
_____
_____

End of the Day Reflections

Top 3 Goals for the Day
_____
_____
_____
_____
_____
_____
_____

TODAY: _____

NOTES:

What did you dream about last night?
_____
_____
_____
_____
_____
_____
_____

Today's " Get It Done" List
_____
_____
_____
_____
_____
_____
_____

End of the Day Reflections

Top 3 Goals for the Day
_____
_____
_____
_____
_____
_____
_____

TODAY: _____   NOTES:

What did you dream about last night?

Today's "Get It Done" List

Top 3 Goals for the Day

End of the Day Reflections

TODAY: _____   NOTES:

What did you dream about last night?

Today's " Get It Done" List

End of the Day Reflections

Top 3 Goals for the Day

TODAY: _____   NOTES:

What did you dream about last night?

Today's " Get It Done" List

Top 3 Goals for the Day

End of the Day Reflections

TODAY: _____

NOTES:

What did you dream about last night?
_____
_____
_____
_____
_____
_____
_____

Today's " Get It Done" List
_____
_____
_____
_____
_____
_____
_____

End of the Day Reflections

Top 3 Goals for the Day
_____
_____
_____
_____
_____
_____
_____

TODAY: _____   NOTES:

What did you dream about last night?
_____
_____
_____
_____
_____
_____

Today's " Get It Done" List
_____
_____
_____
_____
_____

End of the Day Reflections

Top 3 Goals for the Day
_____
_____
_____

TODAY: _____

NOTES:

What did you dream about last night?

Today's " Get It Done" List

Top 3 Goals for the Day

End of the Day Reflections

TODAY: _____   NOTES:

What did you dream about last night?

Today's " Get It Done" List

End of the Day Reflections

Top 3 Goals for the Day

TODAY: _____

NOTES:

What did you dream about last night?

Today's " Get It Done" List

End of the Day Reflections

Top 3 Goals for the Day

TODAY: _____   NOTES:

What did you dream about last night?

Today's " Get It Done" List

End of the Day Reflections

Top 3 Goals for the Day

TODAY: _____

NOTES:

What did you dream about last night?

Today's " Get It Done" List

Top 3 Goals for the Day

End of the Day Reflections

TODAY: _____

NOTES:

What did you dream about last night?
_____
_____
_____
_____
_____
_____
_____

Today's " Get It Done" List
_____
_____
_____
_____
_____
_____

End of the Day Reflections

Top 3 Goals for the Day
_____
_____
_____
_____
_____
_____
_____

TODAY: _____   NOTES:

What did you dream about last night?
_____
_____
_____
_____
_____
_____
_____
_____

Today's " Get It Done" List
_____
_____
_____
_____
_____
_____
_____

End of the Day Reflections

Top 3 Goals for the Day
_____
_____
_____
_____
_____
_____
_____

TODAY: _____   NOTES:

What did you dream about last night?
_____
_____
_____
_____
_____
_____
_____

Today's " Get It Done" List
_____
_____
_____
_____
_____
_____
_____

Top 3 Goals for the Day
_____
_____
_____
_____
_____
_____
_____

End of the Day Reflections

TODAY: _____   NOTES:

What did you dream about last night?
_____
_____
_____
_____
_____
_____
_____

Today's " Get It Done" List
_____
_____
_____
_____
_____
_____
_____

End of the Day Reflections

Top 3 Goals for the Day
_____
_____
_____
_____
_____
_____
_____

TODAY: _____   NOTES:

What did you dream about last night?

Today's " Get It Done" List

End of the Day Reflections

Top 3 Goals for the Day

TODAY: _____

NOTES:

What did you dream about last night?

Today's "Get It Done" List

End of the Day Reflections

Top 3 Goals for the Day

TODAY: _____ NOTES:

What did you dream about last night?

Today's " Get It Done" List

Top 3 Goals for the Day

End of the Day Reflections

TODAY: _____ NOTES:

What did you dream about last night?
_____
_____
_____
_____
_____
_____
_____
_____

Today's " Get It Done" List
_____
_____
_____
_____
_____
_____
_____

End of the Day Reflections

Top 3 Goals for the Day
_____
_____
_____
_____
_____
_____
_____

TODAY: _____   NOTES:

What did you dream about last night?
_____
_____
_____
_____
_____
_____
_____

Today's " Get It Done" List
_____
_____
_____
_____
_____
_____
_____

End of the Day Reflections

Top 3 Goals for the Day
_____
_____
_____
_____
_____
_____
_____

TODAY: _____ NOTES:

What did you dream about last night?
_____
_____
_____
_____
_____
_____
_____

Today's " Get It Done" List
_____
_____
_____
_____
_____
_____
_____
_____

Top 3 Goals for the Day
_____
_____
_____
_____
_____
_____
_____
_____

End of the Day Reflections
_____
_____
_____
_____
_____
_____
_____
_____

TODAY: _____   NOTES:

What did you dream about last night?
_____
_____
_____
_____
_____
_____
_____
_____

Today's " Get It Done" List
_____
_____
_____
_____
_____
_____
_____

Top 3 Goals for the Day
_____
_____
_____
_____
_____
_____
_____
_____

End of the Day Reflections

TODAY: _____

NOTES:
_____
_____
_____
_____
_____
_____
_____
_____
_____
_____
_____
_____
_____
_____

What did you dream about last night?
_____
_____
_____
_____
_____
_____
_____

Today's " Get It Done" List
_____
_____
_____
_____
_____
_____
_____
_____

End of the Day Reflections
_____
_____
_____
_____
_____
_____
_____
_____
_____

Top 3 Goals for the Day
_____
_____
_____
_____
_____
_____
_____

TODAY: _____   NOTES:

What did you dream about last night?

Today's " Get It Done" List

End of the Day Reflections

Top 3 Goals for the Day

TODAY: _____   NOTES:

What did you dream about last night?
_____
_____
_____
_____
_____
_____
_____
_____

Today's " Get It Done" List
_____
_____
_____
_____
_____
_____
_____

End of the Day Reflections

Top 3 Goals for the Day
_____
_____
_____
_____
_____
_____
_____

TODAY: _____

NOTES:

What did you dream about last night?

Today's " Get It Done" List

Top 3 Goals for the Day

End of the Day Reflections

TODAY: _____

NOTES:

What did you dream about last night?

Today's " Get It Done" List

End of the Day Reflections

Top 3 Goals for the Day

TODAY: _____   NOTES:

What did you dream about last night?
_____
_____
_____
_____
_____
_____
_____

Today's " Get It Done" List
_____
_____
_____
_____
_____
_____

End of the Day Reflections

Top 3 Goals for the Day
_____
_____
_____
_____
_____

TODAY: _____   NOTES:
                                        _____
What did you dream about last night?   _____
_____   _____
_____   _____
_____   _____
_____   _____
_____   _____
_____   _____
_____   _____
                                        _____
       Today's " Get It Done" List   _____
_____   _____
_____   _____
_____   _____
_____   End of the Day Reflections
_____   _____
_____   _____
_____   _____
        Top 3 Goals for the Day   _____
_____   _____
_____   _____
_____   _____
_____   _____
_____   _____
_____   _____

TODAY: _____

NOTES:

What did you dream about last night?

Today's " Get It Done" List

End of the Day Reflections

Top 3 Goals for the Day

TODAY: _____	NOTES:

What did you dream about last night?

Today's " Get It Done" List

End of the Day Reflections

Top 3 Goals for the Day

TODAY: _____   NOTES:

What did you dream about last night?
_____
_____
_____
_____
_____
_____

Today's " Get It Done" List
_____
_____
_____
_____
_____
_____

End of the Day Reflections

Top 3 Goals for the Day
_____
_____
_____
_____
_____

TODAY: _____ NOTES:

What did you dream about last night?
_____
_____
_____
_____
_____
_____
_____

Today's " Get It Done" List
_____
_____
_____
_____
_____
_____
_____

Top 3 Goals for the Day
_____
_____
_____
_____
_____
_____
_____

End of the Day Reflections

TODAY: _____   NOTES:

What did you dream about last night?
_____
_____
_____
_____
_____
_____
_____

Today's " Get It Done" List
_____
_____
_____
_____
_____
_____
_____

End of the Day Reflections

Top 3 Goals for the Day
_____
_____
_____
_____
_____
_____

TODAY: _____

NOTES:

What did you dream about last night?

Today's " Get It Done" List

End of the Day Reflections

Top 3 Goals for the Day

TODAY: _____   NOTES:

What did you dream about last night?
_____
_____
_____
_____
_____
_____
_____

Today's " Get It Done" List
_____
_____
_____
_____
_____
_____

End of the Day Reflections

Top 3 Goals for the Day
_____
_____
_____
_____
_____
_____

TODAY: _____   NOTES:

What did you dream about last night?
_____
_____
_____
_____
_____
_____
_____

Today's " Get It Done" List
_____
_____
_____
_____
_____
_____
_____

Top 3 Goals for the Day
_____
_____
_____
_____
_____
_____
_____

End of the Day Reflections

TODAY: _____   NOTES:

What did you dream about last night?

Today's " Get It Done" List

End of the Day Reflections

Top 3 Goals for the Day

TODAY: _____   NOTES:

What did you dream about last night?
_____
_____
_____
_____
_____
_____
_____

Today's " Get It Done" List
_____
_____
_____
_____
_____
_____
_____

Top 3 Goals for the Day
_____
_____
_____
_____
_____
_____
_____

_____
_____
_____
_____
_____
_____
_____
_____
_____
_____

End of the Day Reflections
_____
_____
_____
_____
_____
_____
_____
_____
_____

TODAY: _____   NOTES:

What did you dream about last night?
_____
_____
_____
_____
_____
_____
_____

Today's " Get It Done" List
_____
_____
_____
_____
_____
_____
_____

Top 3 Goals for the Day
_____
_____
_____
_____
_____
_____
_____

End of the Day Reflections

TODAY: _____   NOTES:
_____
What did you dream about last night?
_____
_____
_____
_____
_____
_____
_____

Today's " Get It Done" List
_____
_____
_____
_____
_____
_____
_____

End of the Day Reflections

Top 3 Goals for the Day

TODAY: _____

NOTES:

What did you dream about last night?
_____
_____
_____
_____
_____
_____

Today's " Get It Done" List
_____
_____
_____
_____
_____
_____

End of the Day Reflections

Top 3 Goals for the Day
_____
_____
_____
_____
_____
_____

TODAY: _____   NOTES:

What did you dream about last night?
_____
_____
_____
_____
_____
_____
_____

Today's " Get It Done" List
_____
_____
_____
_____
_____
_____
_____

Top 3 Goals for the Day
_____
_____
_____
_____
_____
_____
_____
_____

_____
_____
_____
_____
_____
_____
_____
_____
_____
_____
_____

End of the Day Reflections
_____
_____
_____
_____
_____
_____
_____
_____
_____
_____
_____

TODAY: _____   NOTES:

What did you dream about last night?
_____
_____
_____
_____
_____
_____
_____

Today's " Get It Done" List
_____
_____
_____
_____
_____
_____

End of the Day Reflections

Top 3 Goals for the Day
_____
_____
_____
_____
_____
_____

TODAY: _____   NOTES:

What did you dream about last night?
_____
_____
_____
_____
_____
_____
_____
_____

Today's " Get It Done" List
_____
_____
_____
_____
_____
_____
_____

Top 3 Goals for the Day
_____
_____
_____
_____
_____
_____
_____

End of the Day Reflections

TODAY: _____   NOTES:

What did you dream about last night?

Today's " Get It Done" List

End of the Day Reflections

Top 3 Goals for the Day

TODAY: _____ NOTES:

What did you dream about last night?
_____
_____
_____
_____
_____
_____
_____
_____

Today's " Get It Done" List
_____
_____
_____
_____
_____
_____

End of the Day Reflections

Top 3 Goals for the Day
_____
_____
_____
_____
_____
_____

TODAY: _____   NOTES:

What did you dream about last night?

Today's " Get It Done" List

End of the Day Reflections

Top 3 Goals for the Day

TODAY: _____

What did you dream about last night?
_____
_____
_____
_____
_____
_____
_____

Today's " Get It Done" List
_____
_____
_____
_____
_____
_____

Top 3 Goals for the Day
_____
_____
_____
_____
_____
_____

NOTES:
_____
_____
_____
_____
_____
_____
_____
_____
_____
_____
_____
_____

End of the Day Reflections
_____
_____
_____
_____
_____
_____
_____
_____

TODAY: _____   NOTES:

What did you dream about last night?
_____
_____
_____
_____
_____
_____
_____

Today's " Get It Done" List
_____
_____
_____
_____
_____
_____
_____

Top 3 Goals for the Day
_____
_____
_____
_____
_____
_____
_____
_____

End of the Day Reflections

TODAY: _____   NOTES:

What did you dream about last night?

Today's " Get It Done" List

End of the Day Reflections

Top 3 Goals for the Day

TODAY: _____   NOTES:

What did you dream about last night?
_____
_____
_____
_____
_____
_____
_____

Today's " Get It Done" List
_____
_____
_____
_____
_____
_____
_____

Top 3 Goals for the Day
_____
_____
_____
_____
_____
_____
_____

End of the Day Reflections

TODAY: _____

What did you dream about last night?
_____
_____
_____
_____
_____
_____
_____

Today's " Get It Done" List
_____
_____
_____
_____
_____
_____
_____

Top 3 Goals for the Day
_____
_____
_____
_____
_____
_____
_____

NOTES:
_____
_____
_____
_____
_____
_____
_____
_____
_____
_____
_____
_____

End of the Day Reflections
_____
_____
_____
_____
_____
_____
_____
_____

TODAY: _____   NOTES:

What did you dream about last night?
_____
_____
_____
_____
_____
_____
_____

Today's " Get It Done" List
_____
_____
_____
_____
_____
_____
_____

End of the Day Reflections

Top 3 Goals for the Day
_____
_____
_____
_____
_____
_____
_____

TODAY: _____ NOTES:

What did you dream about last night?

Today's " Get It Done" List

End of the Day Reflections

Top 3 Goals for the Day

TODAY: _____   NOTES:

What did you dream about last night?
_____
_____
_____
_____
_____
_____
_____
_____

Today's " Get It Done" List
_____
_____
_____
_____
_____
_____
_____

End of the Day Reflections

Top 3 Goals for the Day
_____
_____
_____
_____
_____
_____
_____
_____

TODAY: _____

NOTES:

What did you dream about last night?

Today's " Get It Done" List

Top 3 Goals for the Day

End of the Day Reflections

TODAY: _____

NOTES:

What did you dream about last night?

Today's " Get It Done" List

Top 3 Goals for the Day

End of the Day Reflections

TODAY: _____   NOTES:

What did you dream about last night?
_____
_____
_____
_____
_____
_____
_____

Today's " Get It Done" List
_____
_____
_____
_____
_____
_____

End of the Day Reflections

Top 3 Goals for the Day
_____
_____
_____
_____
_____
_____

TODAY: _____

NOTES:

What did you dream about last night?

Today's " Get It Done" List

Top 3 Goals for the Day

End of the Day Reflections

TODAY: _____   NOTES:

What did you dream about last night?
_____
_____
_____
_____
_____
_____
_____

Today's " Get It Done" List
_____
_____
_____
_____
_____
_____
_____

End of the Day Reflections

Top 3 Goals for the Day
_____
_____
_____
_____
_____
_____
_____

TODAY: _____   NOTES:

What did you dream about last night?
_____
_____
_____
_____
_____
_____
_____

Today's " Get It Done" List
_____
_____
_____
_____
_____
_____

End of the Day Reflections

Top 3 Goals for the Day
_____
_____
_____
_____
_____
_____

TODAY: _____   NOTES:

What did you dream about last night?
_____
_____
_____
_____
_____
_____
_____
_____

Today's " Get It Done" List
_____
_____
_____
_____
_____
_____
_____

Top 3 Goals for the Day
_____
_____
_____
_____
_____
_____
_____
_____

End of the Day Reflections

TODAY: _____   NOTES:

What did you dream about last night?
_____
_____
_____
_____
_____
_____
_____

Today's " Get It Done" List
_____
_____
_____
_____
_____
_____

Top 3 Goals for the Day
_____
_____
_____
_____
_____
_____

End of the Day Reflections

TODAY: _____   NOTES:

What did you dream about last night?
_____
_____
_____
_____
_____
_____
_____

Today's " Get It Done" List
_____
_____
_____
_____
_____
_____
_____

Top 3 Goals for the Day
_____
_____
_____
_____
_____
_____
_____

End of the Day Reflections

TODAY: _____   NOTES:

What did you dream about last night?

Today's " Get It Done" List

End of the Day Reflections

Top 3 Goals for the Day

TODAY: _____   NOTES:

What did you dream about last night?
_____
_____
_____
_____
_____
_____
_____

Today's " Get It Done" List
_____
_____
_____
_____
_____
_____
_____

Top 3 Goals for the Day
_____
_____
_____
_____
_____
_____
_____

End of the Day Reflections

www.ingramcontent.com/pod-product-compliance
Lightning Source LLC
Chambersburg PA
CBHW051806100526
44592CB00016B/2579